©2013, from *Heirloom Miniature Quilts* (AQS, 1990)

GENERAL INSTRUCTIONS

The instructions given here are not meant to be complete, "how to make a quilt from scratch" information. There are many books written on that subject already in the marketplace. The directions included here are for the purpose of instructing the quiltmaker in creating historically accurate miniature quilts.

CHALLENGES

Designing a miniature quilt requires the same considerations and decisions as those of a full-size quilt. If the miniature is being designed for use on a specific doll bed, however, some additional issues arise.

Doll beds, old and new, come in many sizes and shapes, and require the quilt to fit them perfectly, if it is to be successful. In other words, a well-done heirloom miniature is one that in a photograph would be indistinguishable from a large quilt. The miniature should drape and fold softly like a large quilt, should have a focal point, interest over the pillow area, and include borders that enhance and do not simply "end off" the quilt.

For doll bed quilts, I have developed a technique to produce on paper the proportions of the finished quilt. First, the quiltmaker must construct all the bedding that will go on the doll bed (mattress(es), pillow(s), blanket, etc.). After these have been placed on the bed, measurements can be made of the various spaces that will be contained in the finished quilt.
Measure:
A. length of bed from headboard to footboard
B. width of bed from side to side of mattress
C. "tuck in" at the head of the bed, depth and width
D. "tuck in" at the foot of the bed, depth and width
E. distance from top of mattress to "floor" or however long you want the sides to be. (See Figures 1 & 2.)

Draw each of these sets of measurements (Figure 3).

All the dimensions of the design areas of the quilt are now visible and it is easy to plan the specific size blocks necessary to fill these spaces. No need to fret over whether a 3" block for the border will work; the quiltmaker only needs to look at the side areas on her plan to know the answer.

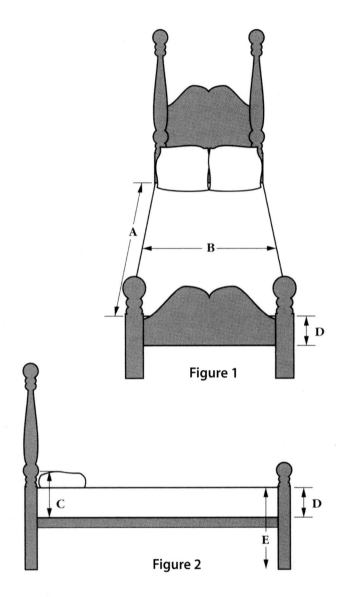

Figure 1

Figure 2

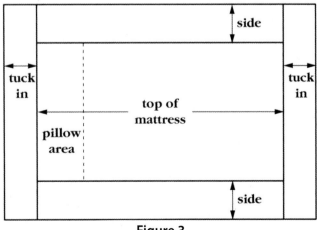

Figure 3

Just as for doll bed quilts, a miniature quilt planned for the wall should be exciting and dynamic as well as balanced and in proportion if it is to be successful. By using the paper diagram technique, it is easy to plan a patchwork or appliqué pattern to fit any size doll bed or wallhanging.

FABRIC
Weight and Weave:
Loose weaves and gauze-like fabrics are usually unsuitable for miniature work. When handling pieces of fabric 1" square or smaller, fraying can become a problem and the additional difficulty of handling a loose weave can make your project more frustrating than fulfilling. If you must insist on such a type of fabric for color reasons, etc., then use the paper-piecing construction technique. This method stabilizes your fabric.

Stay away from heavy-weight fabrics such as wools and corduroys. These fabrics tend to be stiff and hard to handle when piecing or doing appliqué. In addition, the resulting quilt will be very stiff and will not drape or fold properly over a miniature doll bed. If your small quilt is for a wall, then a heavier weight fabric might be suitable.

Do use medium-weight, good quality, 100-percent cotton fabrics. These handle well and tend to have a minimum of fraying problems. By keeping all the fabrics you use in one quilt the same weight, you will find that your piecing and appliqué work will go more smoothly and look better.

Always wash the fabric that you will be using in your project in hot water with a good quality soap. I like to wash my fabrics in Orvus®, which is recommended for safe use on old fabrics. But no matter what soap you are using, be sure to thoroughly rinse your fabric to remove all soap residue. This residue can remain in your fabrics and cut their life span. You will be spending many hours making an heirloom miniature; don't let shortcuts destroy your work.

Surface Design:
It would seem logical that I would suggest small prints, but large prints are not to be overlooked. A quilt composed of prints that are all the same size or scale can become very boring. Large prints can provide extra interest by drawing attention to certain areas or features of the quilt. They can also add drama to the overall effect of the completed quilt. Since these quilts are small, special effects can be achieved by using the fabric surface designs.

A special trick available to miniature quiltmakers is the use of one or two large prints to provide the look of many different fabrics. For example, if a large flower print is used (Figure 4) and a clear template measuring 1" square is placed on the fabric and moved around to different areas, many different options for pattern and color emerge.

An additional advantage of using fabric this way is that all the pieces cut from the same cloth will recombine effectively in the quilt. The reason for this is simple: the manufacturer of the cloth had already designed these shapes and colors to blend together. All the quiltmaker has to do is move them around and create new shapes and patterning.

Figure 4

All surface designs are suitable in miniature—flower patterns, squiggly lines, geometric shapes, and wide or narrow stripes. Each of these has its own special use. Pinstripes can be used in the pinwheel pattern to make the blades appear to spin. Wide stripes can be cut apart to create sashings or borders. Geometric shapes can be used to represent objects that the manufacturer never intended.

In order to help you better visualize the possibilities of a piece of fabric, try cutting a 1" square of clear plastic to take along with you on buying trips to the quilt store. When you get there, place the square on the fabric you are considering and move it around the surface to see what shapes and objects you can discover. In this way, you will find that one-half yard of fabric can be equal to many different pieces of fabric without the additional cost!

Color:

Keep the color scheme for a miniature quilt simple. Too many different colors within the small size of these quilts makes it hard for the eye to focus and enjoy the design and workmanship of the quilt. Do not feel that only two or three colors per quilt is proper, either. Often fabric of only two colors can look flat and uninteresting when used alone in a quilt.

The easiest way to determine a color scheme is to select a multi-color print fabric. This type of fabric provides the quilt with a third dimensional effect, even without the quilting that will come later, and can be the source of the colors that will compose the quilt. For example, using an overall print fabric that has green vines, flowers in two shades of salmon, blue-purple flowers, and yellow or gold centers on a light green background provides many colors to be drawn out and used throughout the entire quilt.

Include highlight and accent colors within your quilt. A miniature is not really different from a a large quilt when it comes to color; the same rules apply.

I do not give "the" colors to use with each pattern in the "how to" section. The reason for this is that I believe each quiltmaker should use the color choices that most please her or him. A project is more likely to be finished if it pleases its maker. If you feel that you need some direction for starting your miniature, use the color photographs of each quilt as a guide for fabric selection.

TEMPLATES

I like to use plastic for my templates. I prefer the "see through" types so that I can be sure to center the designs accurately on each pattern piece. Window templates of metal or cardboard also work well.

Since we are quilters, we tend to make our templates by cutting the shapes out with scissors. I find that there can be too much wobble or variation when using scissors. I prefer to use a craft knife and a metal ruler and over-cut each side of the template. If you do not try to cut through the plastic all at once, but rather score the lines (by repeating several times), the template will drop out and be very accurate without any nicks or bumps.

Be sure to measure and mark all templates very accurately. The width of a pencil line can be critical when working in miniature. I recommend using a mechanical pencil of 5mm width or finer for marking the template plastic. An error of 1⁄16" over only 16 pieces becomes a full one inch discrepancy, a large error on a quilt that only measures 16"!

CONSTRUCTION TECHNIQUES

Cut strips the desired width and length from your fabric. Sew the strips together in pairs or larger quantities as each quilt requires (Figure 5). The arrows indicate the direction of the machine stitching; by sewing alternately up and down, you can reduce warpage of the unfinished blocks.

PIECING

Whether piecing by machine or hand in the traditional assembly fashion or by quick-piecing techniques, I always use a standard 1⁄4" seam. I do not trim the seams after construction except where multiple seams come together, such as at a star's mid-point, where I grade the seams and cut off any excess. I like to leave the standard 1⁄4" seams because I feel it gives additional strength to the quilts.

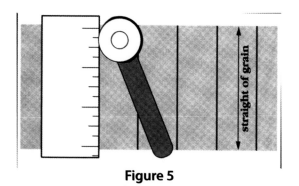

Figure 5

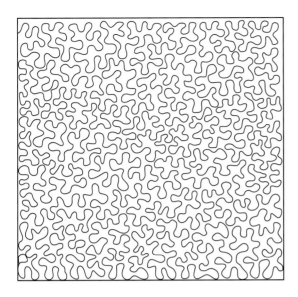

Stipple quilting
Figure 13

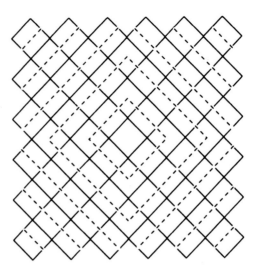

Figure 14

Since seams are a problem in these quilts, one is tempted to forego large amounts of quilting. I think this approach is in error. It is the quilting that makes a quilt a quilt. And it is the quilting that adds depth and dimension to any patchwork or appliqué design. Since the purpose is to capture the look and essence of an old quilt, it is important to remember that the originals were heavily quilted. To duplicate them, as much quilting as possible should be included in the miniature.

When hand quilting a miniature with small appliqué such as the Oak Leaves (pg. 20) or when embroidered vines or stems are next to the quilting, be sure to consider the proportion between the quilting stitches and the work. Not everyone can quilt small enough (18 stitches or more to the inch) to keep the quilting stitches in scale with the appliqué or embroidery. Whenever I'm faced with this problem, I often only quilt close to the edge of the small work so that the quilting isn't immediately noticeable. The result is that I have provided the quilting the miniature needs without confusing the eye as to where it should focus, the designs or the quilting.

I also find it confusing to the eye when contrasting color quilting thread is used. I always match my quilting thread to the background area or patch that I am quilting. This way the quilting becomes secondary to the design surface of the quilt, as in full-size quilts, and allows the viewer to fully and more carefully enjoy the work.

TYING
Originally many quilts were not made as bedspreads or counterpanes but as blankets for warmth, a strictly utilitarian purpose. As a result many quilts received no quilting but instead were tied. Wool yarn was used to make knots at even intervals across the quilt to hold the three layers together. There is no reason not to apply this technique to a miniature quilt. I have used it on hexagon and log cabin quilts.

Sometimes I like the ties to show and do knotting on the front (Log Cabin Variation) with three strands of embroidery floss. Other times, as with the hexagons, I only use the tying to hold the layers together and use one or two strands of floss, knotting on the reverse side where it won't interfere with the graphic design of the top.

FINISHING TECHNIQUES
A. Backing brought over front:
Bring the backing fabric over the front edge of the quilt and tuck in the edges of the backing to form a ¼" wide binding, trimming the backing fabric as necessary. For a professional look, miter all binding corners.

B. Tucking edges in:
Turn in front and back edges of quilt to the inside and slip stitch the edges together. Be sure to trim the batting ¼" narrower than the front and backing so that it will fit nicely inside the edge without buckling.

C. Alternatives:

Use a separate binding, made either of straight of grain or bias strips.

Insert piping in between the front and back edges of the quilt. I have seen this technique used on quilts from the mid-and-late-19th century. Be sure to keep the piping in scale with the size of the quilt. The hand-loomed tapes used on the late 18th and early 19th century quilt edges can be imitated by the use of binding on a loose-weave fabric. Trim the quilt to even the edges, and apply the binding over both the top and back surfaces of the quilt using a running stitch. End off by cutting the binding ½" longer than needed, then fold the raw edge to the inside, and slipstitch the end of binding edge over the beginning edge.

The scalloped edges that were popular in the 1920s and 30s can also be achieved if care is taken in their planning.

Prairie points can be folded to fit a miniature quilt's edge.

Use old lace or handmade tatting to simulate the handmade fringes of the late 18th and early 19th century quilts. Many of these quilts were white-on-white counterpanes and would look excellent on a four-poster doll bed.

Any edge or finishing treatment used on a large quilt can be used on a miniature, just remember to keep it in scale with your quilt.

SIGNING AND DATING

I'm a firm believer in signing and dating all quilts and quilted objects that a quilter makes. How easy our quilt heritage research projects would be if all the quiltmakers of the past had signed and dated their quilts! There is no reason not to sign your work. Be proud of what you have produced, and if your work is a gift for someone, they will be proud to have your name on it.

I always put my name, date, copyright symbol if appropriate, and number in the series on the back of each quilt, no matter what the size. Some of the quilts are embroidered with the information (Figure 15). Others are written in indelible ink on a separate label. I prefer, when possible, to mark directly on the quilt; a separate label can always get lost.

In order to further document my work, I keep a 5½" x 8" three-ring notebook with my original graphs, fabric swatches, and all pertinent information (beginning and completion dates, number in the series, photos of each quilt, etc.) This log or "bible" will afford future historians a wealth of information, not only about the quilts but about their maker as well, and it will provide me with documented proof for my insurance company in case of an accident or theft claim.

It only takes a few minutes while you are making a quilt to write down the facts, but it can take ever so much longer if you wait until after the quilt is complete to try and remember all the information you will need to write down in your log. So stop right now, and buy a three-ring notebook for recording your work! Future quilt historians will thank you.

Figure 15

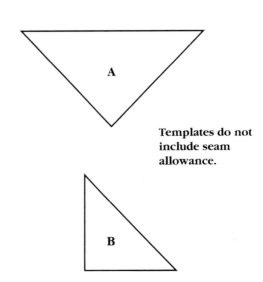

GEESE IN FLIGHT, 19" x 24", made by the author

SKILL LEVEL: *Beginner*

Dimensions: 19" x 24"
Number of pieces: 278
Construction technique: pieced, hand, or machine
Fabrics: scraps, stripe for sashing and border

DIRECTIONS:

Stitch patch A to both B's to produce block unit (Figure 16). Stitch five rows of 18 geese each. Add sashings to geese rows. Add borders, mitering the corners. Quilt all rows in the ditch along sashings and border edges. Complete quilt using finishing technique A (page 9).

OPTIONAL:

Quilting may be done around individual geese.

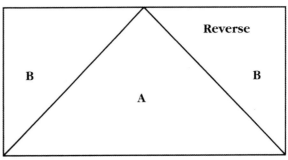

Figure 16

Templates do not include seam allowance.

YARDAGE:

Assorted scraps
Sashings and border - ¾ yard
Backing - ¾ yard

CUT:

90 A
90 B
90 B in reverse
2 strips 18½" x width of narrow stripe plus seam allowance for sashings
2 strips 18½" x width of wide stripe plus seam allowance for sashings
2 strips 24½" x width or stripe plus seam allowance for side borders
2 stripes 10" plus width of sashings, plus seam allowance for top and bottom borders
1 rectangle 21" x 26", backing

NINE-PATCH, 15½" x 18½", made by the author

SKILL LEVEL: *Beginner*

Dimensions: 15½" x 18½"
Number of pieces: 320
Construction techniques: pieced, rotary cutter, and sewing machine
Fabrics: strong contrast between fabrics A & B and C & Z. Medium contrast for solid blocks and half-triangle border.

YARDAGE:

A & inner border - ¼ yard
B - ⅜ yard
C - ¼ yard
Z - solid blocks & outer border - ¼ yard
V & W - border triangles & backing - ⅝ yard

CUT:

7 strips 1" wide of A
7 strips 1" wide of C
9 strips 1¼" wide of B
7 strips 1" wide of B
3 strips 1¼ wide of A
3 strips 1¼ wide of C
20 squares 2¼" of Z
18 triangles of W
4 triangles of V
2 strips 1" x 15" of inner border
2 strips 1" x 18" of inner border
2 strips 1¼" x 20" of outer border
2 strips 1¼" x 18" of outer border
1 rectangle 18" x 21" of backing

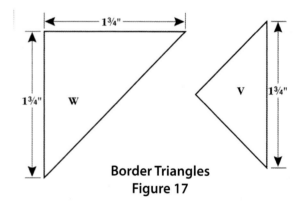

Border Triangles
Figure 17

Templates do not include seam allowance.

Z
Template

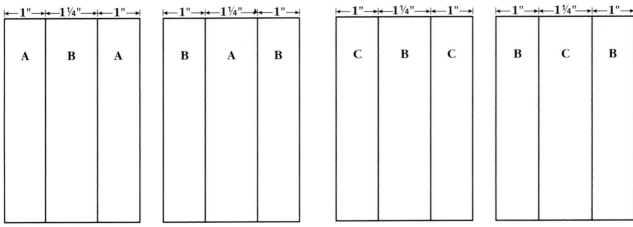

Figure 18

Figure 19

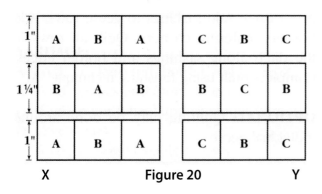

X   Figure 20   Y

Assemble pieced blocks alternately with solid blocks Z, attaching triangles to the ends of each row. See assembly diagram (Figure 21). Add borders, mitering corners. Quilt all rows in the ditch and extend quilting lines through solid blocks, forming a nine-patch shape in each block. Complete quilt using finishing technique A (page 9).

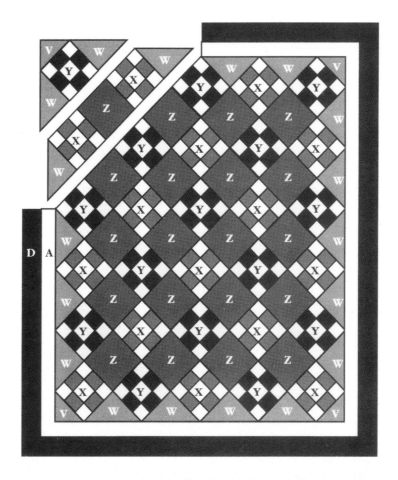

Figure 21

FRIENDSHIP, 25½" x 31", made by the author

YARDAGE:

B - Scraps or fat quarters of many different prints.
A - Background color in each block - ⅝ yard.
C - Muslin centers - ¼ yard
Sashing and top triangles (D) - ½ yard
Side and bottom triangles (E) - ⅜ yard
Backing & binding - 1 yard

CUT:

196	A	5	D
196	B	13	E
49	C	4	F

Sashings: 1 strip 1¼" x 33½" (piecing when necessary)
              1 strip 1¼" x 29¾"
              1 strip 1¼" x 26"
              1 strip 1¼" x 22¼"
              1 strip 1¼" x 18½"
              1 strip 1¼" x 14¾"
              1 strip 1¼" x 11"
              1 strip 1¼" x 7¼"
              40 strips 1¼" x 3½"

SKILL LEVEL: *Intermediate*

Dimensions: 25½" x 31"
Number of Pieces: 511
Construction Techniques: pieced, hand or machine
Fabrics: scraps or fat quarter, sashing and top triangles should contrast well with blocks, outside triangles should be slightly darker than sashings; backing– striking or complex pattern to add interest, richness, and age; also used as binding.

DIRECTIONS:

Assemble block units (Figure 22). Sign and date "c" blocks, if desired, using a fine-point indelible pen, such as a permanent Pilot™ marker. Sew short sashing strips between blocks. Sew long sashings to bottom of each assembled row. Use the assembly diagram, (Figure 23), for sashing and row construction.

When assembled, the tip of the D triangles will extend beyond sides of quilt. Trim them to square off corners.

Quilting: Quilt in the ditch around all pattern pieces and sashing seams. Quilt inside border triangles ⅝" from seams in a chevron pattern; repeat shape ⅝" from previous row, (Figure 24).

Complete quilt using finishing technique A (page 9).

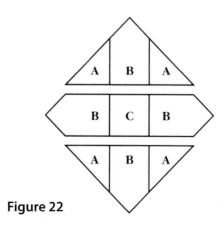

Figure 22

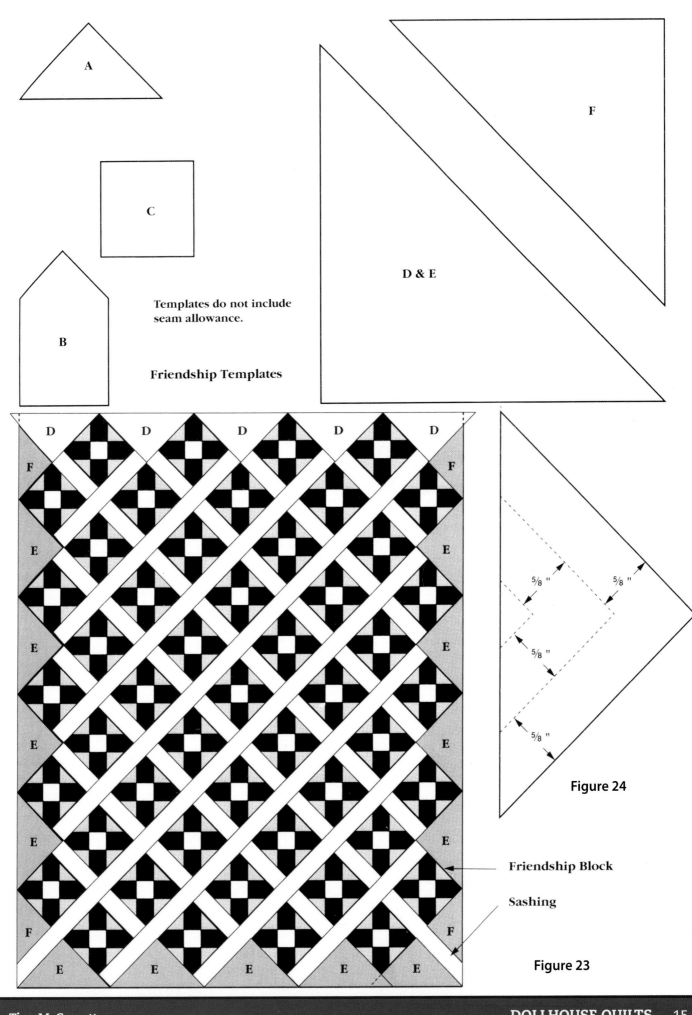

A

C

B

Templates do not include
seam allowance.

Friendship Templates

D & E

F

Figure 24

⁵⁄₈ "   ⁵⁄₈ "

⁵⁄₈ "

⁵⁄₈ "

D   D   D   D   D

F   F

E   E

E   E

E   E

E   E

E   E

Friendship Block

Sashing

F   F

E   E   E   E   E

Figure 23

CRAZY, 18" x 13½", made by the author

YARDAGE:
Scraps or ¼ yard of 9 different fabrics .
¾ yard of backing fabric
¼ yard of lightweight muslin

CUT:
3 strips 3½" x 18½" muslin
20" x 26" rectangle of backing fabric
2 strips 1½" x 18½" for sashings
4 strips 3½" x 18" for borders

Cut various fabrics from templates, trying not to make two alike so as to give more interest to the quilt.

SKILL LEVEL: *Beginner to Intermediate*

Dimensions: 18" x 13½"
Number of pieces: 54
Construction techniques: appliqué
Fabrics: light and medium-weight velvet, sateen moire, taffeta, ribbons, silks. Purchased embroideries may be used either with or instead of doing fancy embroidery designs.

DIRECTIONS:
To each of the three muslin strips, stitch the patches in the sequence provided in the row assembly diagram (Figure 25, page 18). Place the resulting strips so that the two outside rows are in the same top to bottom order and reverse the top and bottom order for the middle row.

Attach the completed strips to the sashing strips, using the quilt photo as a guide. Add side borders, then top and bottom borders. It is not necessary to miter the corners.

Embroidery: Using two strands of embroidery floss and the embroidery stitches shown opposite, embroider over all seam lines. Laces and trims can be hand or machine stitched to the seam lines if you do not wish to embroider. Using the special embroidery designs provided, fill in the crazy patches with your choice of designs and colors. Don't hesitate to be creative and invent or vary standard stitches. Add embroidery designs that come in packages from fabric stores, or old or new laces, etc. Experiment, that is what CRAZY quilts are all about!

Quilting: Traditionally, crazy quilts are not quilted because there isn't any batting placed inside them. You can take a few tacking stitches to keep the back and front from separating, if desired.

Complete the quilt using finishing technique A (page 9).

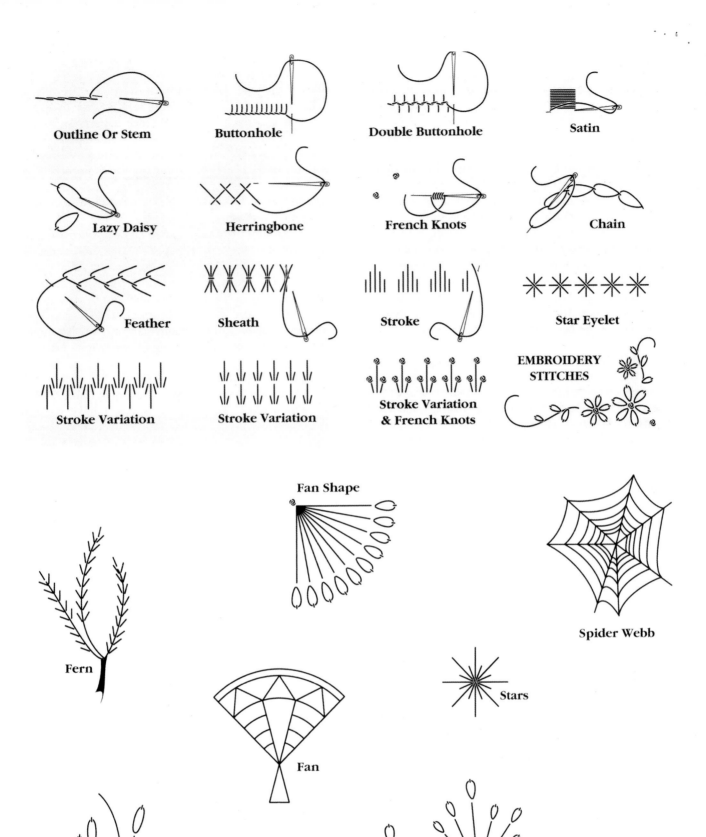

Outline Or Stem

Buttonhole

Double Buttonhole

Satin

Lazy Daisy

Herringbone

French Knots

Chain

Feather

Sheath

Stroke

Star Eyelet

Stroke Variation

Stroke Variation

Stroke Variation & French Knots

EMBROIDERY STITCHES

Fan Shape

Spider Webb

Fern

Stars

Fan

Cattails

Flowers

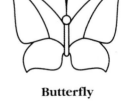

Butterfly

Top

Bottom

Figure 25
Row assembly

Center line

Center line

Crazy Quilt templates
Templates do not include seam allowances.

SUMMER GARDEN

SKILL LEVEL: *Beginner*

Dimensions: 19½" x 20½"
Number of pieces: 512
Construction techniques: English paper piecing
Fabrics: 5 different prints for a soft old look, OR 5 solids for a contemporary look.

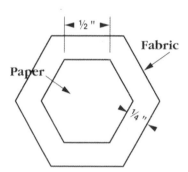

SUMMER GARDEN template

SUMMER GARDEN, 19½" x 20½", made by the author

YARDAGE:
⅝ yard of A (includes backing)
¼ yard of B
¼ yard of C
¼ yard of D
½ yard of E

CUT:
142 hexagons of fabric A
20 hexagons of fabric B
184 hexagons of fabric C
126 hexagons of fabric D
40 hexagons of fabric E
22" x 23" rectangle of fabric A for backing
512 papers (copy the SUMMER GARDEN template.)

DIRECTIONS:
Fold fabric over papers and baste as described in the English paper piecing instructions (page 5). Assemble into rosettes from the center out (Figure 26). If you do not want a jagged hexagon-shaped edge, appliqué the edges of all sides of the quilt to a narrow band of fabric A. After the top is assembled, remove the papers.

Because of all the seams, no batting is necessary. It will drape more softly without it.

Tie with a single strand of embroidery floss in square knots on the reverse side.

Complete quilt using finishing technique A (page 9).

A ⬢ B ⬡ C ⬡ D ⬢ E ⬡

Figure 26

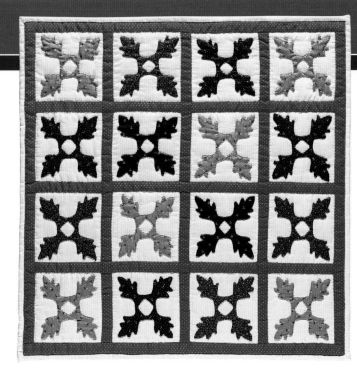

OAK LEAVES

SKILL LEVEL: *Intermediate*

Dimensions: 17" x 17"
Number of pieces: 48
Construction technique: Appliqué and pieced
Fabrics: 4 different greens
white for backing and squares
red or other color for sashings

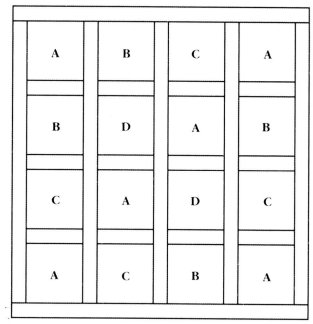

Figure 27 Quilt top assembly

OAK LEAVES, 17" x 17", made by the author

YARDAGE:

greens –   A - ¼ yard   B - ¼ yard
            C - ¼ yard   D - ¼ yard
Backing and squares – ⅝ yard
Sashings – ½ yard

CUT:

16 – 4" squares
1 – 19" square for backing
2 strips 17" x 1"
5 strips 16" x 1"
12 strips 4" x 1"
6 leaves of A
4 leaves of B
4 leaves of C
2 leaves of D

DIRECTIONS:

Appliqué each leaf onto one of the 4" squares. Using Figure 27 as an assembly guide, sew a short sashing strip to the bottom of the first three squares in each vertical row. Attach the 16" long sashings to the sides of all rows. Add the two 17" long strips to top and bottom of quilt to complete borders.

Quilting: Quilt around each leaf pattern and along the sashings and borders in the ditch. Complete quilt using finishing technique A (page 9).

Oak Leaf template
Template does not include seam allowance.

Yo-Yo

SKILL LEVEL: *Beginner*

Dimensions: 9½" x 11½"
Number of pieces: 238
Construction technique: Yo-Yos (see page 6)
Fabrics: dark - A
           medium - B
           medium light - C
           light - D

DIRECTIONS:

Using assembly diagram (Figure 28) for color placement, make the quilt by assembling yo-yos in pairs on the reverse. Use matching color thread and a whipstitch. After each row is constructed, press lightly with iron. Assemble rows. No batting or quilting is needed. Quilt is complete. A lining may be added to the reverse, if desired.

Yo-Yo, 9½" x 11½", made by the author

YARDAGE:

A – ¼ yard B – ¼ yard
C – ¼ yard D – ¼ yard

CUT:

Cut circles 1¾" in diameter as follows:
  40 A
 106 B
  52 C
  40 D

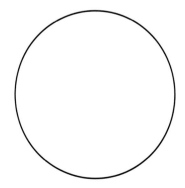

Yo-Yo Template
Template includes seam allowance.

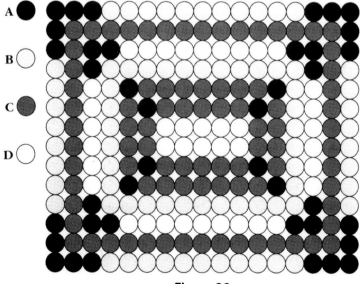

Figure 28

ONE-PATCH SCRAP

One-Patch Scrap, 20" x 20", made by the author

SKILL LEVEL: *Beginner*

Dimensions: 20" x 20"
Number of pieces: 421
Construction technique: pieced
Fabrics: all colors and in varying intensities (light, medium, dark)

DIRECTIONS:

Assemble the squares in rows, staggering the placement of colors and the light and dark intensities. Row 1 is made of 29 squares. Each subsequent row pairs will diminish by 2 squares; that is, rows 2A and 2B contain 27 squares, rows 3A and 3B contain 25 squares, etc. (See Figure 29.) The edges will be zigzag-shaped and can be cut straight using ruler and rotary cutter or scissors.

Quilting: Quilt in the ditch around center square and through the middle of the next squares forming a diamond shape. Continue in this fashion until the entire surface has been completed.

Complete quilt using finishing technique A (page 9).

YARDAGE:

Scraps
⅝ yard for backing

CUT:

421 1½" squares
22" square for backing

One-Patch Scrap template
Template does not include
seam allowance.

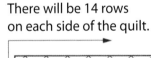
There will be 14 rows
on each side of the quilt.

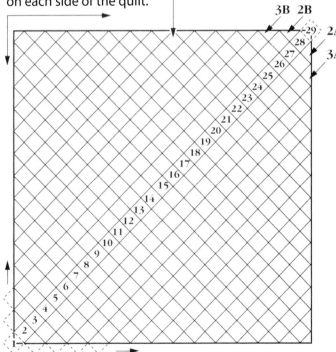

Trim excess from blocks to
make a smooth edge.

Figure 29

ROSE DREAM, 22" x 25", made by the author

YARDAGE:
½ yard of A
1 yard of B, includes backing

CUT:
42 of template 1 of fabric A
42 of template 1 of fabric B
21 of template 2 of fabric A
21 of template 2 of fabric B
42 of template 3 of fabric A
42 of template 3 of fabric B

Innermost border:
2 strips 1" x 20" of fabric B
2 strips 1" x 23" of fabric B

Middle border:
2 strips 1" x 21" of fabric A
2 strips 1" x 24" of fabric A

Outer border:
2 strips 1" x 23" of fabric B
2 strips 1" x 26" of fabric B

24" x 27" rectangle of B for backing

Papers:
84 of template 1
42 of template 2
84 or template 3

SKILL LEVEL: *Beginner*

Dimensions: 22" x 25"
Number of pieces: 222
Construction technique: paper piecing
Fabrics: two colors, strong contrast

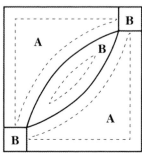 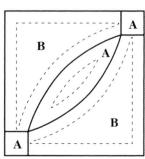

Figure 30

DIRECTIONS:
Cover papers with fabric and prepare as in the English paper piecing directions (page 5). Whipstitch pieces together to make block units (Figure 30). Whipstitch pieces together in rows, alternating units until there are six across and seven rows down. Add borders, mitering corners.

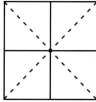

Quilting: Quilt around pattern pieces 1 and 2, ¼" inside seam lines. Quilt diagonally through corner squares 3 (Figure 31).

Figure 31

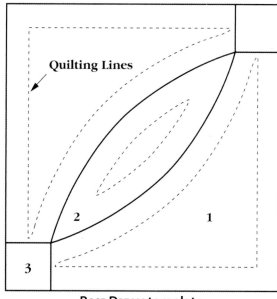

ROSE DREAM template
Actual size of the paper templates
Add seam allowance to fabric templates

PRINCESS FEATHER, 20" x 20", made by the author

SKILL LEVEL: *Intermediate*

Dimensions: 20" x 20"
Number of pieces: 314
Construction technique: appliqué and pieced
Fabrics: 2 contrasting colors, prints or solids, and light or neutral for background

DIRECTIONS:
Alternating colors, appliqué feathers to the background. Piece star and appliqué over feather stems. Appliqué circle over star center. Cut away excess fabric from back of appliqué work. Piece border blocks and attach to sides (Figure 32).

Quilting: Quilt around all appliqués and along seam lines in stars and border pieces. Quilt background in diagonal rows ¼" apart throughout background and into light triangles in outside border. Quilt ¼" inside seam lines in triangular-shaped areas in the outside row of border (Figure 32).

Complete quilt using finishing technique A (page 9).

YARDAGE:
¾ yard of fabric A (includes backing)
⅜ yard of fabric B
⅜ yard of fabric C

CUT:
1 template 1 of fabric A
8 template 2 of fabric B
4 template 3 of fabric A
4 template 3 of fabric B
76 template 4 of fabric A
148 template 4 of fabric B
72 template 4 of fabric C
4 template 5 of fabric A
16½" square for background
22" square for backing

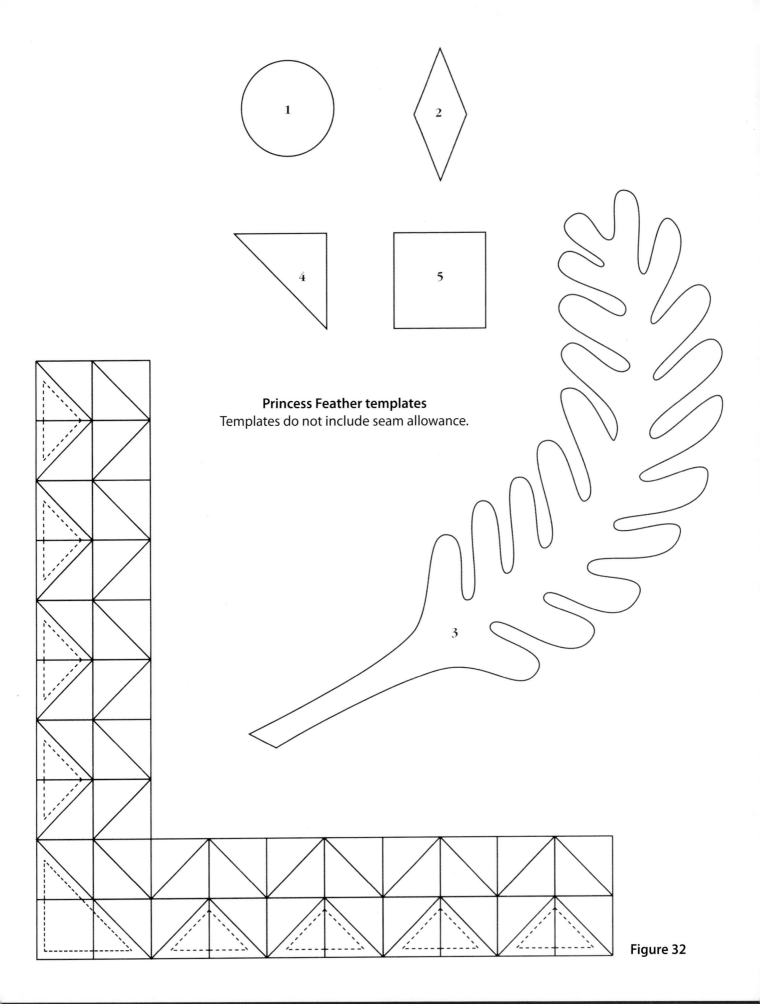

Princess Feather templates
Templates do not include seam allowance.

1

2

4

5

3

Figure 32

KAMIKANI KAILI ALOHA, 20" x 20", made by the author

HAWAIIAN "KAMAKANI KAILI ALOHA"

SKILL LEVEL: *Advanced*

Dimensions: 20" x 20"
Number of pieces: 3
Construction technique: appliqué
Fabrics: strong contrasting solid colors

DIRECTIONS:

Using the 20" square of A, fold and press into quarters and then eighths (see Figure 9, page 6). Place pattern piece 1 on folded fabric with diagonals and straight edges of fabric along dotted lines on patterns. The point, X, should be at the point of the folded fabric. Trace around the template and add ³⁄₁₆" seam allowance (Figure 33). Repeat this procedure for pattern piece 2. Carefully cut out the shapes with SHARP scissors. Do not unfold until time to baste onto background square. Unfold carefully, DO NOT PRESS.

Using the 20" square of fabric B (background), fold and press as before. Place the center motif on the background, carefully aligning the diagonals, being careful not to stretch the appliqué out of shape. Repeat for the border motif. Using thread to match the motif, stitch in place starting with the inside cut out areas. Keep your stitches small and even. At tight turnings, clip and adjust width of seam allowances and closeness of your stitches, as necessary. After the appliqué is complete, carefully press the top.

Quilting: Echo quilting is a traditional Hawaiian technique. Quilt around the appliqué designs close to edges. Then quilt ¼" inside and outside the appliqué, following the appliqué's shape. Continue in like manner until the entire surface is covered.

Complete quilt using finishing technique A (page 9).

YARDAGE:

⅝ yard of A – appliqué and backing
⅝ yard of B – background

CUT:

1 – 20" square of A
1 – 20" square of B
1 – 22" square of A (backing)

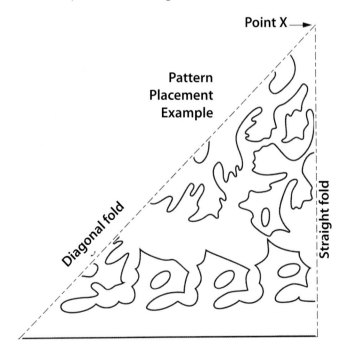

Point X →

Pattern Placement Example

Diagonal fold

Straight fold

Figure 33

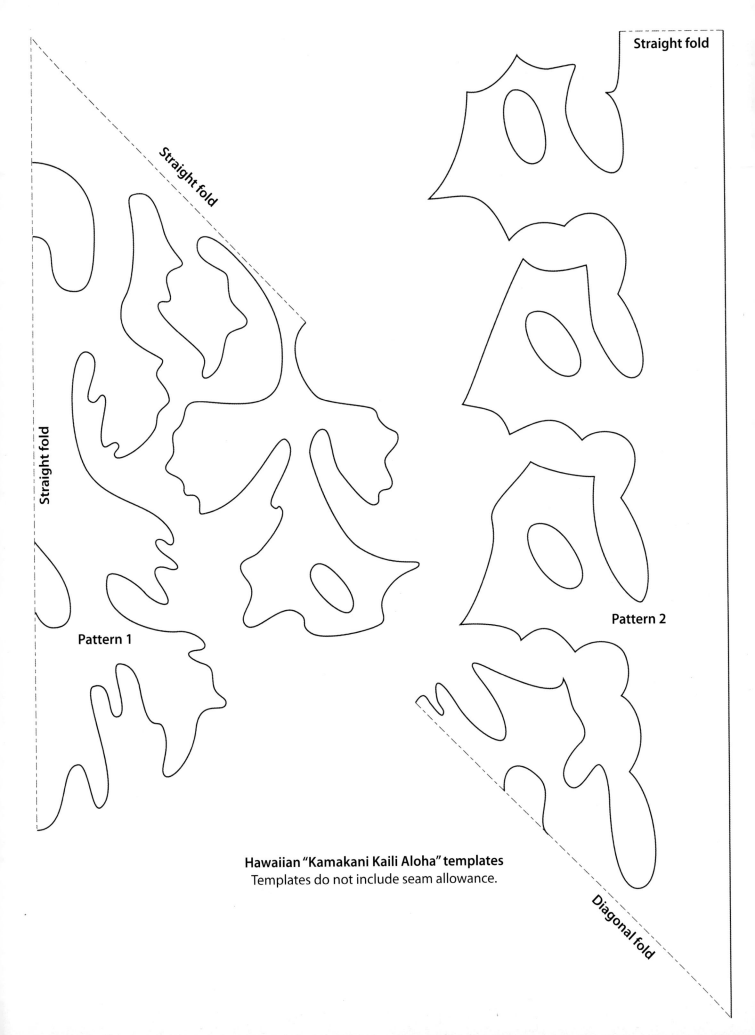

Straight fold

Straight fold

Straight fold

Diagonal fold

Pattern 1

Pattern 2

Hawaiian "Kamakani Kaili Aloha" templates
Templates do not include seam allowance.

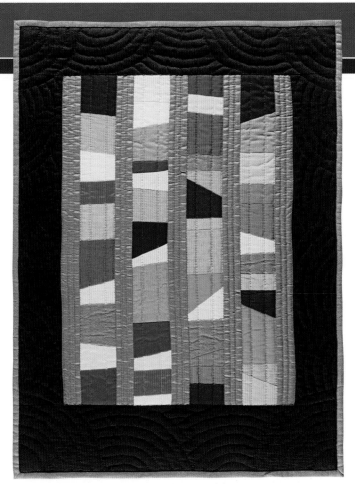

CHINESE COINS

SKILL LEVEL: *Beginner*

Dimensions: 17" x 23"
Number of pieces: 58 (approximate)
Construction technique: pieced
Fabrics: 19 different solids

DIRECTIONS:

Sew the many patchwork pieces together forming four rows, each 18½" long. Attach these rows to the sashing strips. Next attach side and top borders. Add the wide border strip to bottom.

Quilting: Quilt two rows ¼" apart through center of sashing strip. In pieced rows, quilt two parallel rows the length of the strip ½" from seam lines (Figure 34).

For borders, use clamshell quilting patterns provided (Figure 35).

Complete quilt using finishing technique A (page 9).

CHINESE COINS, 17" x 23", made by the author.

YARDAGE:

scraps or remnants
¼ yard for sashings
¼ yard for borders
¾ yard for backing

CUT:

1 strip 2½" x 17½" for top border
2 strips 2½" x 18½" for side borders
1 strip 3½" x 17½" for bottom border
5 strips 1½" x 18½" for sashings
19" x 25" rectangle for backing
strips of 17 different solids, 2½" wide and varying widths at different angles.

Figure 34

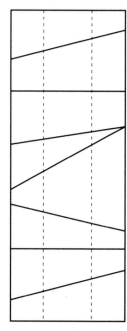

Figure 35

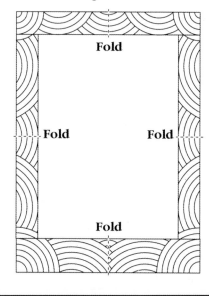

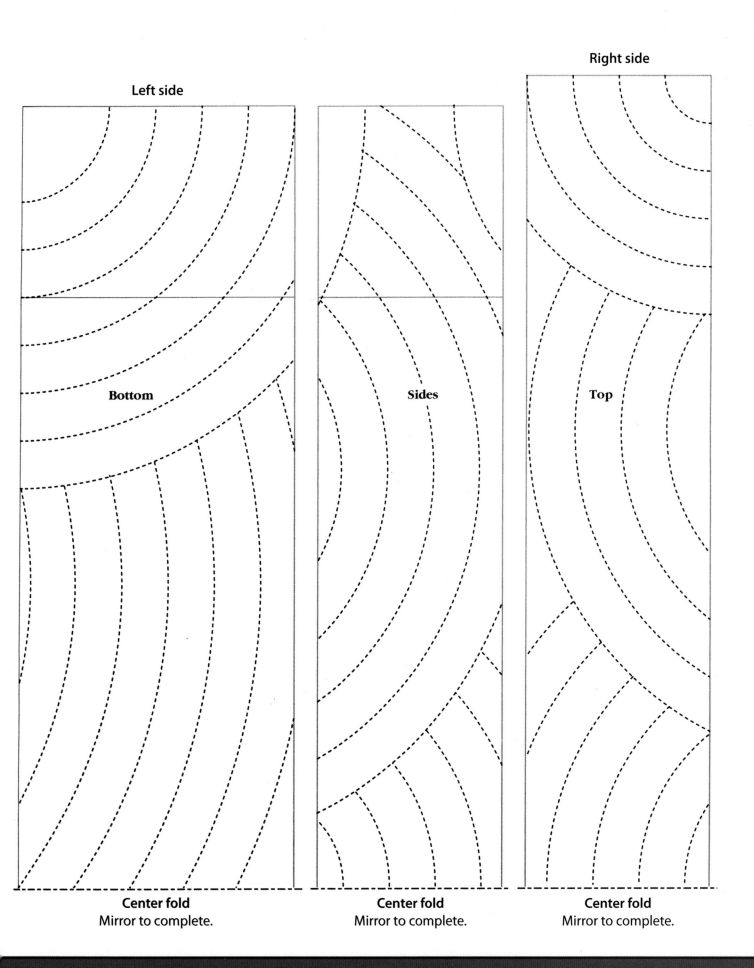

Left side

Right side

Bottom

Sides

Top

Center fold
Mirror to complete.

Center fold
Mirror to complete.

Center fold
Mirror to complete.

GRANDMOTHER'S FANS, 18" x 22", made by the author

SKILL LEVEL: *Intermediate*

Dimensions: 18" x 22"
Number of pieces: 200
Construction technique: pieced
Fabrics: scraps or a planned color scheme

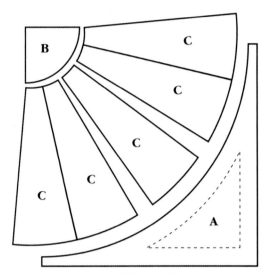

Figure 36

YARDAGE:
¾ yard – A (includes backing)
⅛ yard – B
scraps – C
⅜ yard – D – borders

CUT:
 28 – A
 28 – B
140 – C
2 strips 3½" x 28½" from fabric D
2 strips 3½" x 22½" from fabric D
20" x 24" rectangle from fabric A

DIRECTIONS:
Assemble the fan blocks by piecing in units (Figure 36).
Sew the blocks together in diagonal rows; see assembly
diagram (Figure 37). Add borders and miter corners.

Quilting: Quilt all the seams in the ditch. In the arc over
the fan, quilt ¼" inside seam lines, echoing the arc shape
(Figure 36). Using the cable quilting pattern, quilt the
borders.

Complete quilt using finishing technique A (page 9).

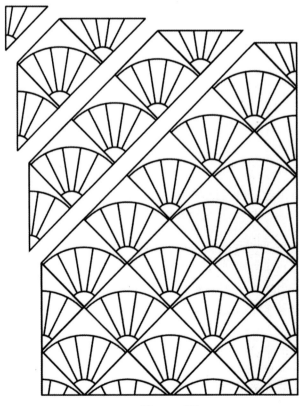

Figure 37

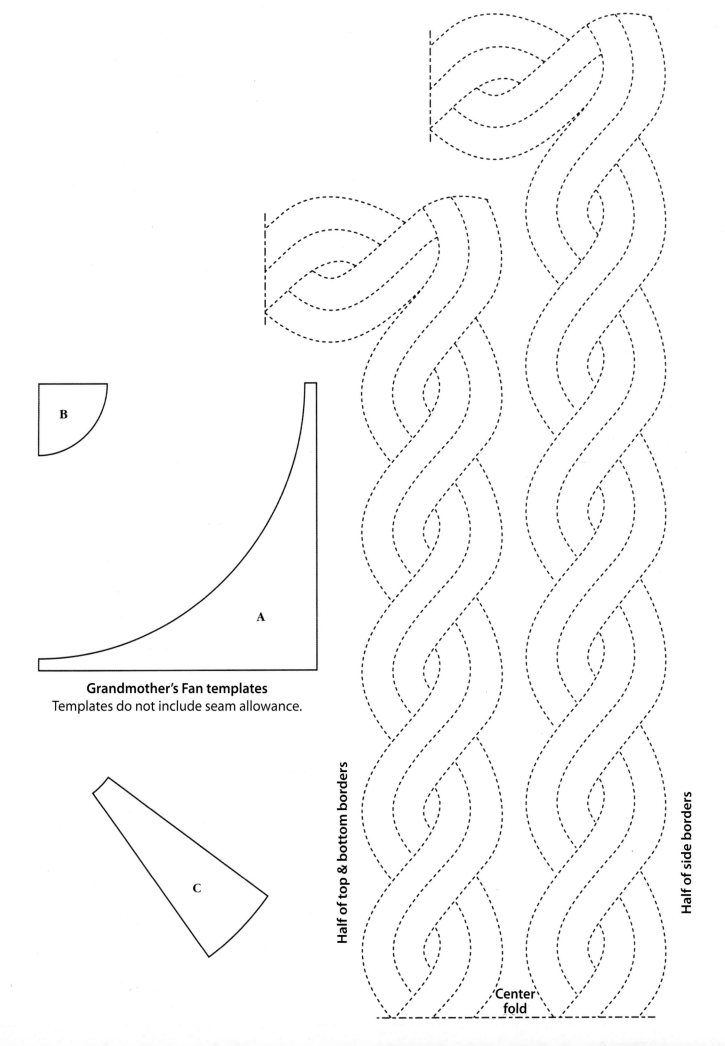

Grandmother's Fan templates
Templates do not include seam allowance.

B

A

C

Half of top & bottom borders

Half of side borders

Center
fold

More AQS Books

This is only a small selection of the books available from the American Quilter's Society. AQS books are known worldwide for timely topics, clear writing, beautiful color photos, and accurate illustrations and patterns. The following books are available from your local bookseller, quilt shop, or public library.

#1284

#1288

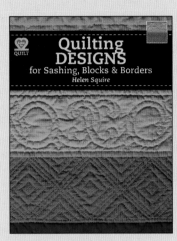

#1286

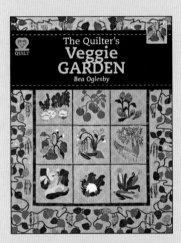

#1287

#1292

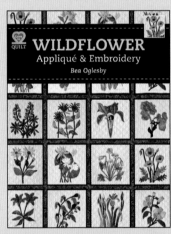

#1289

#1293

#1295

#1297

LOOK for these books nationally.
CALL or **VISIT** our website at

1-800-626-5420
www.AmericanQuilter.com